WEALT NG

AS PRACTICED BY THE
WORLD'S RICHEST PEOPLE

What the Kuwaitis Can Teach You about Getting Rich—and Staying Rich

Paladin Press • Boulder, Colorado

William Beaver

Wealth-Building Secrets as Practiced by the World's Richest People:
What the Kuwaitis Can Teach You about Getting Rich—and Staying Rich
by William Beaver

Copyright © 1998 by William Beaver

ISBN 0-87364-976-1
Printed in the United States of America

Published by Paladin Press, a division of
Paladin Enterprises, Inc., P.O. Box 1307,
Boulder, Colorado 80306, USA.
(303) 443-7250

Direct inquiries and/or orders to the above address.

PALADIN, PALADIN PRESS, and the "horse head" design
are trademarks belonging to Paladin Enterprises and
registered in United States Patent and Trademark Office.

All photographs courtesy of the Kuwait Ministry of Information.

Table of Contents

For Suhair, Jacob, and Jasmin.

This book is also dedicated to the people who have made an indelible impression on my attitudes about money and wealth: Bassam Hassounah, Tom Remlinger, Jim Watt, and Matt Young. Each in his own way has shown me what's possible.

Acknowledgments

This book is the result of many people giving me their encouragement, valuable time, and hard-won knowledge. Special thanks to Ala Salem Al-Qattan and Abdul Rahman Abdul Hameed Al-Hmoud, for their historical background information on Kuwait's business community, and to all the people at the Al-Mulla Group.

Waffa Al-Rushaid from the Kuwait Stock Exchange gave me tremendous help. Claudia Farkas Al-Rashoud is a fellow American author and photographer here in Kuwait, who sets the standard for the rest of us. Barron Hall, my poker buddy and long-term American expat, is actually a Philippine land tycoon disguised as a mild-mannered computer expert.

Andrew Hutton shared his research on the Kuwaiti *diwaniya*. I always appreciate the valuable advice of Ernest Alexander, both as my attorney and as my friend. Ayman Al-Harmi, from the National Bank of Kuwait, will probably surprise me one day by owning half of Nuzha.

And finally, thanks to all of my extended family, both in Kuwait and America. I hope someday you better understand why I do what I do.

Introduction

Poverty is often a state of mind induced by a neighbor's new car.

—Anonymous

Have you ever found yourself thinking, "I want to be rich"? Did you ever say to yourself, "If only I had more money"? If so, you probably have asked yourself, "*How* do I make more money"? With a wife and young children to support, I find myself thinking about these things quite often. And I know I'm not alone.

The world has become obsessed with the idea that we all need more money. We tell ourselves a little more is all we need to be happy. We spend so much time thinking about the *how* of making money, we give very little time to the *why*. Why be rich? Why have money?

If someone walked up to you tomorrow and handed you a million dollars, what would you do? More important, what would you do differently than you are doing now? Think about it for a moment.

"I'd buy a house or a car or take a vacation," you might answer. So, why can't you do that now? What could you do with a million dollars that you can't do right this minute? Usually the answers deal with size, not with the principle. You can donate to charity now, but probably not a new wing for your local hospital. You can buy a car now, but it probably wouldn't be a Mercedes. You could take a vacation now, but it probably wouldn't be a world cruise in a first-class cabin. You could buy a house now, but it might not be a mansion.

In the West, we are taught very early, by a variety of teachers, that money offers freedom: from the usual handcuffs of time, since money can give us the time to do what we really want; from the restraints that keep us tied down in one place, since money gives us the ability to travel and have more than one home if we want; and from the worry about being held hostage financially, since lots of money in the bank offers financial security.

In fact, making money is not very difficult. You may have to spend time learning a new way of thinking about money, but once you've learned the basic principles, you may find yourself angry that you didn't start long ago. And once you figure out how to make a hundred, you'll find a way to make a thousand.

But strangely enough, when we do make more money, we usually find plenty of ways for our life-style to grow. We move on to a bigger, more expensive car or home. We take that vacation we've always wanted. Before we know it, we're back hovering at the break-even line, usually unable to save for our future or our children's future.

Instead of working toward the freedoms we want—those of time and financial security—we fritter away our money. Instead of making the money work for us, we end up right back working for the money. We find ourselves standing in front of the shaving mirror, wishing we could be one of the lucky ones, believing that life handed them something we didn't get. We wipe away the steam, mumbling to ourselves, "If only I could win the lottery."

Now try to imagine an entire country winning the lottery. Fantastic maybe, but this is what many people think when they talk about oil-rich Middle Eastern countries, especially Kuwait. Twenty years ago, nobody had even heard of the tiny emirate at the top of the Persian Gulf. But because of the American reflagging of Kuwaiti oil tankers during the Iran-Iraq war, and then the war to liberate Kuwait from the Iraqis, the country is now fairly familiar to most people. Unfortunately, so are the rumors.

The words *lucky, rich, spoiled,* and *wealthy* are often used to generalize the Kuwaiti people. Like most stereotypes, there is only the

In the early days of Kuwait, fresh water had to be imported. Here a water merchant signs for his full water bladders, which he will then sell door to door. (All photographs courtesy of the Kuwait Ministry of Information.)

smallest grain of truth to these descriptions. Being married to the daughter of a former Kuwaiti ambassador, and running a successful business in Kuwait, I should know.

Long before the discovery of oil, which only by good fortune proved to be 10 percent of the world's reserves, the merchants of Kuwait had already earned a reputation as tough, shrewd businessmen, master boat builders, and expert pearl divers. Kuwaiti wealth builders had long ago learned to take

Now part of Kuwait's fresh water is stored in large water towers.

advantage of their circumstances. They found themselves in the middle of the route linking Great Britain and Europe to India and the Orient, a geographic fact that provided many opportunities, such as being providers and protectors of overland caravans.

As I mentioned, Kuwait enjoyed the distinction of having the finest boat builders and pearl-diving crews in the region. Many people became rich as pearl merchants and many more by selling the supplies such crews needed.

Long ago, Kuwaitis were known as expert shipbuilders.

Others became wealthy as traders, especially when you consider that even everyday commodities, such as fresh water, had to be imported by boat from Basra, Iraq.

Traders and merchants by definition had to learn how to make a profit, and profit means delayed gratification. Instead of using the money to buy something for their immediate gratification, the merchants and traders opted to use the money to buy something they could sell for a higher price later. Then they would take the difference and do it again.

Looking closely at the wealth-building tactics of the Kuwaitis, you see many other general principles at work that are written

One of the main ways of earning money in old Kuwait was pearl diving. Here modern Kuwaitis keep the art of diving for pearls alive.

about in modern personal finance books as if these authors had suddenly stumbled upon, or created, great secrets for amassing wealth. In this book, I will show you that individual circumstances change with the demands of a certain era, but not the actual principles of wealth building.

Many Kuwaitis did become rich because of the discovery of oil and the sudden explosion of money that came with it. But for all the people who became rich, there were nearly as many who made and then quickly lost their wealth. Some employed the secrets of their merchant heritage to preserve and increase their fortunes. Others adopted outrageous lifestyles, which eventually made them bankrupt.

There are many rich families in Kuwait whose wealth comes from several previous generations, but even so, that wealth must still be preserved, protected, and nurtured. Kuwaitis pass on their businesses, and the family wealth, to their sons and nephews, their daughters and wives, but these relatives must learn the discipline of money like anyone else. A million dollars can be lost as easily as a thousand.

Wealth is of course relative at any given point in history. How many Renaissance noblemen, who controlled vast lands and fortunes, knew the joys of indoor plumbing? The old families of Kuwait were rich enough to finance entire fleets of fishing vessels, but in a land that can reach 130 degrees Fahrenheit in the summer, none of these wealthy families enjoyed air conditioning. The size of the numbers, and what they buy, may change from generation to generation, but the basic rules of building wealth stay the same.

There have been countless books written about how to get wealthy or get rich quick. The libraries are filled with books about personal finance and wealth through investing. But just for a moment, stop looking for that one deal that's going to stuff your bank account with cash. Use your common sense and think for yourself about how you accumulate money. If you don't count on winning the lottery or receiving a large inheritance,

The Kuwaitis found themselves on a major trade route that started at the sea . . .

then the "timeless" principles of wealth-building can be easily understood:

1. *Start with the money you already have—whether from a job, a business, an inheritance, or whatever your income source.*
2. *Spend less money than you make.*
3. *Put the difference to work making more money.*
4. *Protect your assets and your money-making abilities.*

If there is a magic formula to building personal wealth, this is it. We tend to think that there must be better, faster, easier ways of doing just about anything, especially making money, but, frankly, there aren't. Each of

. . . and then continued overland.

these four steps has its own problems and
solutions, which we will explore in this book.

What changes from country to country, and
perhaps generation to generation, are individual
tactics and situations. For example, investing in
the U.S. stock market is far more complicated
than in the Kuwait stock market simply because
in Kuwait you have only 66 stocks from which
to choose.

But there is one wealth-building strategy
of the Kuwaitis that you cannot use. This formula was offered sarcastically by one of
America's richest men, Andrew Carnegie,
who said, "If you want to become rich, go to
bed early, get out of bed early, and strike oil."
He was joking, but the Kuwaitis said, "O.K.,
why not?"

CHAPTER ONE

Start from Where You Are

Spend some, save some, give some.

—John Wesley

I came to Kuwait in 1991, married the daughter of a former Kuwaiti ambassador, and then returned for a year to Los Angeles. During that year, my wife and I decided to return to Kuwait. For the first few months, I kept thinking of all the stories I had heard about the immigrants who came to the United States to make a fresh start. They arrived in the old days at Ellis Island, or now at JFK International, and within a few years, they owned a chain of restaurants. I found myself wondering if I could do the same thing in post-Desert Storm Kuwait.

Kuwait is not designed to be an entrepreneurial country in the same mold as the United States. Much of the prosperity enjoyed by the Kuwaitis begins with government spending of oil revenue, but a considerable portion of the wealth is created by large merchant families. In part because of Arab tradition, the family structure in Kuwait is much tighter than in the United States. In my own case I have seen my wife and her family go to the aid of her second and third cousins. (I don't even know who my second and third cousins are.) This tradition of large, extended families allows many people with a common interest to privately control large and diverse business interests.

THE ORIGINS OF KUWAIT'S WEALTH

When the Kuwaiti pioneers came from the interior of the Arabian peninsula in the late 18th century, they set up their community on the Northwestern shores of the Persian Gulf (in Kuwait they call it the Arabian Gulf, but I'll use the more common name). Of the original group, the Al-Sabah family became the rulers with the consent of the other eight merchant families who arrived with them. These eight became known as the "heritage families" and now control a great deal of the Kuwaiti economy.

Kuwait in the 1700s demanded the most of its inhabitants, since it was basically a large tract of desert with harsh summertime temperatures reaching 135° Fahrenheit and higher. But from the beginning, those who settled near Kuwait Bay demonstrated a willingness to work hard and make the best of their situation,

The harsh climate demanded the most of Kuwait's early citizens.

not unlike the pioneers in North America who traveled west or the Europeans who set sail for America.

These early Arabian settlers developed the opportunities presented to them by both the geographic locale and their tribal connections

15

The ruler of Kuwait, Sheikh Ahmad Al-Jaber Al-Sabah, with members of British Petroleum (BP) in 1935.

deep in the Arabian peninsula. They found themselves at the nexus of a trade route that linked Britain with the Indian and oriental reaches of its empire. The Kuwaitis took advantage of the situation and soon began leading trade caravans overland. Kuwait, which at the time was referred to as Qurain, eventually became a British protectorate.

During these early years of the country, the merchant mentality of Kuwait developed into a national character. Sons were taught by their fathers in a way similar to that of the guilds of Europe a few centuries ago. The first cardinal rule was *to start from where you are and take advantage of what you can.*

In 1938, the first producing oil well started Kuwait down the road to vast wealth.

The Kuwaitis believe that opportunity always exists if you know where to find it. But to find opportunity and take advantage of it, you need an education. You have to assess what you have working for you. You have to know the way the world works. You have to know how money works.

To teach their sons these lessons, the Kuwaitis trained them in the most mundane details of the family businesses. In fact, the Kuwaitis were the first in the region to send their children abroad for study. But most important to this education was the Arab family structure itself.

Even in modern Kuwait, a father will build

17

Kuwaitis today can either choose to build their own home . . .

a very large house with the intention of his eldest son living in part of it when he is old enough to marry. Some still live in family compounds consisting of large walled-in areas with two or more houses. Almost every day at lunchtime, the family will come together to eat. Other days, the extended family—uncles, aunts, and cousins—will gather together, which over time gives a child a sense of belonging to something larger than himself. Often these large families have traditions and temperaments with which the members proudly identify.

Kuwaitis leave home far later than typical Americans, and some never move out at all. In terms of wealth building, considering that the

. . . or wait for one of the free government-built homes.

largest expenditure for a typical American family is housing, Kuwaitis certainly have an advantage if they stay home. Even if they want to move out, certain advantages exist.

Knowing that Arab pride would refuse free handouts, one method used by the government to ensure that some of the new-found oil revenue made it to the citizens was subsidized housing. Today, a Kuwaiti male can choose between a 70,000 Kuwait dinar (KD)—the equivalent of U.S.$230,000—interest-free loan to build a house, or he can apply for a free government tract house. In either case, the sheer number of young Kuwaitis (45 percent of the population is under 25 years old) creates major problems.

19

In the latter case, there is a 10-year backlog of applications for government housing. In the former, 70,000 KD will not buy a house in Kuwait, and will barely cover the cost of the land on which to build it. Residential real estate is very limited because of the small size of the country and because the oil reserves prevent inhabitation of much of the land. Kuwait uses the metric system, so to put real estate prices in understandable terms, consider the following. One acre has 4,047 square meters. At the time of this writing, a plot of land with 1,000 square meters, or one-fourth of an acre, in most of Kuwait's newer residential areas, costs 75,000 KD (U.S.$247,500) or more. Building a house will easily double or triple that price.

In the years since the discovery of oil, Kuwait has developed into what some call a welfare state because of the benefits passed on to the citizens. This condition of welfare is not the same as in the United States, where much of the money for such a program would come from taxes. There are no personal taxes in Kuwait. The money earned from the sale of oil does not belong to any individual, rather it collectively belongs to the state and, by extension, its citizens. The country's population is approaching two million, but only 750,000 of these are Kuwaiti. The benefits given to these native citizens, especially the males, are impressive.

When a Kuwaiti male marries, for example, he is given an outright gift of 2,000 KD

(U.S.$6,600), which is typically used as a part of the traditional Arab dowry to be paid to a new wife. He can also take a loan of the same amount with very liberal repayment terms. If he is a government employee, he will receive a rent subsidy if he doesn't have his own home or a government house. If the male government employee has children, he will receive a small allowance each month for each child.

There are other benefits. Health care in Kuwait, generally speaking, is free. Kuwaitis also typically buy their groceries at local cooperative societies that pay a rebate at the end of the year. When Kuwaitis retire, they receive a government-paid pension, based on a portion of their working salary, for the rest of their lives. Maybe the best feature of Kuwait, at least in American terms, is that there are no income taxes.

Many people hear of these benefits and immediately say, "Well, of course, if I had all those things, I'd be rich too." But surprisingly, one of the drawbacks of Kuwait, which most citizens will privately acknowledge, is the lack of discipline in personal spending, especially among young men and women. Peer pressure dictates a very conformist mentality, which leads to significant consumer overspending to keep up. The young people of Kuwait are just as debt and credit driven as any American.

I know many people who have nothing left at the end of each month because they have high car payments and spend too much on other high-end goods. Young high school students carry cellular telephones and pagers. The older generation of Kuwaitis, those who were around before the discovery of oil, complain that the modern generation wants everything *now* and has no sense of the future. They argue that the young men and women of Kuwait have no respect for money, spending it as fast as they get it.

One acquaintance of mine is a young man from a very wealthy family whose father wanted him to learn about money's value. My 20-year-old friend drove an expensive sports car, given to him by his father. Soon, another more expensive car attracted his attention, and he went to his father about selling the first car and buying the second. His father presented two options. One, he could sell the first car, and the father would give him the additional money necessary to buy the second. There was a catch, however. The father would not pay to maintain the more expensive car. The young man would have to find a way to do it himself. The second option was to take the proceeds from selling the first car and, with money added by the father, buy a piece of land. Because residential land in Kuwait is so limited, its value will almost certainly increase quickly. The son could sell the land after a year or two and make enough profit to not only buy the more expensive car, but also have the additional cash to maintain it, perhaps even having money left over. The son decided not to wait and took the first option, being more interested in impressing girls than waiting. Not long after, he had an accident and couldn't afford to fix the new car.

The conclusion is obvious: although the Kuwaitis are in a perfect situation to build wealth, especially with all the government help with living costs, a large percentage of the population does not. Those who do manage to build wealth do so because they have been taught about the discipline of money in much the same way successful parents all over the world have taught their children. The one thing consistent in all societies is the simple fact that the value of money is not just learned from the society itself, but from the parents. What you do with your money is often a reflection of what you saw your parents do with theirs.

You must start from where you are and take advantage of what is available to you.

Think about this for a moment: try to remember the first money you ever earned. Picture in your mind that first paycheck. Try to remember the second time you earned any money and the next and so on. Now try to remember where it all went. What do you have to show for it?

Many people let the money slip through their fingers without any regard for the future. They have no idea of what the discipline of money requires, but this is a situation easily remedied.

Kuwaitis believe that the most important element of wealth building is education of all kinds.

Earlier, I mentioned that starting from where you are requires an education, and part of that learning is knowing what you can control and what you can't.

You can set goals and work toward them, but you can't control the emergencies and contingencies that happen along the way. You can't control the future of Social Security or government pensions, but you do have control over the cash you save for your retirement. If you work for someone or some company, you can't control whether you lose your job, but you can control earning other income from additional sources or by starting your own business.

You can't control the tax rate, but you can control your tax payments by knowing that you only have to pay the minimum amount required by law. What is that minimum amount for you? You can't control inflation, but you can choose high-quality investments to offset inflation. You can't control rising costs, but you can control how much you spend, and, more important, how much you save. You can also control the risk of your investments through choice and diversification.

Starting from where you are requires knowing where you want to go and then educating yourself on how to get there. The traditional Kuwaiti merchants teach their children by having them work in the family business and learn the discipline of money—and the first lesson is to live within their means.

CHAPTER TWO

Controlling What You Spend

Money was invented so we could know exactly what we owe.

—Cullen Hightower

According to a recent report by Merrill Lynch, there are about 36,000 millionaires in Kuwait, with a total wealth of $98 billion. A recent book about millionaires in the United States estimates that there are 3.5 million. One big difference between the two sets of millionaires is that, according to the research about the American wealthy, 80 percent have earned that wealth in one generation, while in Kuwait, most of the wealth is inherited from at least one generation earlier.

One feature common to both the older generation of Kuwaiti millionaires and the U.S. millionaires cited in the book is that the majority of both are basically frugal with their money. They tend not to flash their wealth around.

Saving money, reinvesting money, and controlling their spending become unbreakable habits for most millionaires. There are, however, countless tales in Kuwait of men and women who made or inherited money only to quickly squander it on big, fancy cars and large homes full of Italian furniture. In both countries, a common term exists describing those with new money who like to show it off: nouveau riche.

Controlling expenditures starts with knowing where your money goes. Every family faces common expenses, such as food, clothing, housing, transportation, and medical expenses. These expenses that occur every month are the place to start controlling expenses.

FOOD

In Kuwait, most people buy their groceries from their local cooperative society, which pays back part of their purchases at year's end as profit sharing. The government also subsidizes many of the commodities, such as rice and baby formula, keeping bulk prices low. Because of the large size of the typical Kuwaiti family, buying in bulk is also a matter of habit, which generally keeps grocery bills much lower.

Most Kuwaiti homes, especially after the

Iraqi invasion, maintain storage rooms, with large quantities of rice, canned goods, cooking oil, cleaning products, and other nonperishable goods.

Kuwait also has many open-air vegetable markets, where fresh produce is sold at a much lower cost than in the stores. Again, the tendency, even among the wealthy, is to buy in bulk quantities.

Because fish has traditionally played such an important role in the Kuwaiti diet, there are fish markets where the day's fresh catch from the Persian Gulf is sold auction-style. The Kuwaitis love to bargain for prices, so the fish market is always humming and noisy, as the fish vendors try to get good prices.

HOUSING

As discussed in Chapter 1, Kuwaitis often have advantages when it comes to housing, even though the prices are very high. Renting an apartment can also be costly. The main protection for consumers in Kuwait involves rental housing laws that prevent the escalation of rent for five years, with an option for the owner to raise the rent by as much as 100 percent after that period.

The one almost certain benefit of owning a home in Kuwait is the tendency of real estate prices to increase. Very seldom do prices drop, simply because of the high demand for quality housing in good locations.

29

Kuwaitis buy food in bulk, especially fresh foods like vegetables.

TRANSPORTATION

Whether in Kuwait or the United States, transportation is the one area with the greatest potential for savings. Most people overpay for their cars, without consideration of alternatives.

Owning a new luxury car in Kuwait has almost become standard among the post-oil generation. High installment payments for Mercedes, BMWs, Volvos, Lexuses, Cadillacs, Jeep Grand Cherokees, and other expensive cars quickly eat away at a monthly salary. The cars that would identify a seasoned successful businessman in the United States—such as a

A fish auctioneer tries to get the best possible price for his catch.

Lexus, Cadillac, or Jaguar—are driven by college-age people in Kuwait. When this is the case, status symbols have no choice but to continue climbing in value. If a Mercedes is commonplace, what do you drive to show off?

Because many young people are concerned about the car they are seen driving, some have even resorted to tricks to change the cars' appearance. You often see a Mercedes with a different model number attached to the trunk, changing, for example, the Model 200 (locally regarded as a "woman's car") to a 230 or 300, simply by going to the junkyard and taking the nameplate

The fresh fish market is always humming with activity.

off a wrecked model. Another trick to make a car appear newer is to put plastic on the seats and headrests, like what you get when you drive a new car from the showroom.

One of the interesting things about preparing this book was the repeated discussions I had with Kuwaitis who pointed out that the "really wealthy" people in Kuwait don't show off their wealth, driving nondescript cars instead. Although everyone knows the game in Kuwait, it is still played by many, many people. For appearance's sake, some resort to buying cars with license plates from Dubai or other Gulf countries. The implication is that the car was paid for with cash, not monthly installments.

Appearances aside, there are many ways to save money on transportation. The most important way is not to buy a new car. Selling cars is a highly evolved art form, no matter what country you're in. The biggest advantages a car salesman has are the customer's lack of knowledge and insecurity. Many Kuwaitis want to be seen driving expensive cars, so the dealer's main concern is making the payments fit their budget, which often means 50 percent or more of their available income. Of course, other people buy new cars because of the fear of buying a used vehicle that might break down.

If you are willing to buy a used car, especially in Kuwait, you can save serious money. Because prestige in Kuwait is often associated with things that are new or innovative, used-car prices can fail to make sense. As an example, my father-in-law bought a brand-new Cadillac Coupe DeVille in 1993 for about 12,000 KD ($39,600). The same car only four years later has dropped tremendously in value because Cadillac changed the body style, making the older car, at least to Kuwaitis, seem dated. The 1993 Cadillac could easily be purchased today for 3,500 KD ($11,550) or less.

The black hole that accompanies new cars is the financing interest charges. As soon as you drive a new car off the lot, its value drops, depreciation begins, and the interest charges continue to eat away at your cash. By spending your money on a used car, even one that is two years old, you save significantly because so much depreciation has already occurred. Many Kuwaitis take advantage of these facts and buy good-quality used cars, but keep them clean and detailed.

One fact of owning any car in Kuwait is the effect of the harsh desert climate. After a few months, for example, the brilliant black molding on a new car will fade because of the intense summer sun, making the car look used anyway.

Buying a new car because you fear a used one will break down isn't realistic either. The fact that Kuwait, for example, has countless automobile repair shops tends to keep repair prices low. Tow trucks constantly prowl the streets looking for motorists who need assistance. And there is no guarantee that a new car won't break down, so the difference in price is far out of proportion.

Consider these expenses of a new versus a four-year-old used car, even if the used car might require major repairs (these numbers are just to be used as an example):

	New	Used
Purchase price	$20,000	$7,000
Resale in 4 years	$7,000	$4,000
Depreciation lost	$13,000	$3,000
Major repairs	0	$1,500
Interest @ 10%	$2,000	$700
Total cost for 4 years	$15,000	$5,200

Difference after 4 years: $9,800

Even if you bought a car less than four years old, you can still figure out the difference and see that it would be significant.

In their book *The Millionaire Next Door* (Longstreet Press, 1996), Thomas Stanley and William Danko interviewed more than 500 millionaires and surveyed more than 11,000. Their findings make clear the frugal nature of self-made millionaires, at least in the United States (my limited, unscientific research in Kuwait indicates much the same). Among the U.S. millionaires, for example, fewer than 25 percent owned a new car, and fully one-third buy used vehicles instead of new.

INSURANCE

With the exception of automobile and business coverage, insurance doesn't play a large role in financial planning in Kuwait. Part of the reason is the ongoing controversy among Islamic scholars of whether life and health insurance is *haram* (forbidden by God, against God's will). Another factor is the dependence on the state social security system for pensions instead of building private retirement accounts.

Technically speaking, many of the wealthy in Kuwait self-insure, which means that they keep large cash or other financial reserves for protection. After the Iraqi invasion in 1990, many people started keeping their wealth outside Kuwait in foreign banks.

Traditionally, the wealthy in Kuwait, especially those who made their fortunes as profit-taking merchants, prefer to keep more direct control over their investments. Those who have ventured into life insurance tend to stick with forms of term insurance instead of whole-life and universal. Low-cost, straightforward "pure" insurance makes more sense to the merchant minded than using insurance as a means of building financial value. Larger profits can be made putting the money to work in other ways, instead of years in uncertain insurance accounts.

THE BIGGEST LESSON OF CONTROLLING YOUR EXPENSES

Of all the wealth-building secrets you can learn from the Kuwaitis the most important is the steadfast, rock-solid, unbendable belief that all value is negotiable. Kuwait's merchant heritage developed in part because of the large number of foreign countries that traded with Kuwait, which meant considerably different outlooks on value.

Before the existence of a single Kuwaiti currency, the dinar, there were several different types of money used, including the Ottoman Empire lira, the Austrian riyal, the Megidid riyal, the Persian qran, various kinds of Omani and Arabian coins, and Indian rupees. During the old days, much of the commerce in Kuwait, both with its citizens and outside traders, involved bartering one thing for something else: pearls for spices or fish for textiles. The talent for skillful bargaining meant better deals. This tradition continues today in Kuwait, almost as a national sport.

Many of the businesses in Kuwait use fixed prices, and people seem to instinctively know which ones do. Restaurants, grocery stores, and other types of businesses tend not to bargain. Other industries, however, thrive on negotiation. The prices paid for personal services are almost always negotiated. New and used car dealers, bulk food sellers (other than cooperative societies), textile and clothing shops, and other stores all use such a system.

Jewelers and gold shops change their base prices every day, based on the current price of gold published by the government. The price of gold itself is fixed, but the charges for "workmanship" can take the

Expensive, ultramodern shopping centers are popular in Kuwait. The shops contain the latest products and fashions from the United States and Europe.

The old traditional fishing boats have been replaced with modern yachts and pleasure boats.

price of a necklace on a roller-coaster ride of quoted prices from shop to shop. The unwritten law of the Kuwaiti merchant is charge what the market will bear, so it is up to the consumer to bring the price down by bargaining.

Successful bargaining requires understanding the product or service for which you are negotiating. It forces you to pay attention to the market, and to understand the fine art of negotiation. The habit of bargaining starts with the little things, like buying fish or a bulk quantity of nails. When you are a successful haggler with small items, then the war games that take place when bargaining for larger items will seem easy.

Negotiation in Kuwait can take on the atmosphere of a complicated blood sport, and it is in that spirit that many businesspeople have become wealthy. Any price given for a product or service is assumed to be inflated on purpose, so the habit becomes one of getting the price back down to an acceptable level.

Once you have learned to keep your spending well within your means, then you can move on to the next step: putting the difference to work to make more money.

CHAPTER THREE

Develop Many Sources of Income

Wealth is largely a matter of habit.
—John Jacob Astor

What do we mean when we say that we want to get rich quick? Generally speaking, we're talking about large chunks of money made fast. Do you really believe you can become rich overnight? Maybe if your eccentric millionaire great aunt dies on her way home and leaves you everything.

The truth that most rich people know is that wealth is built over time from multiple, diverse sources. When a person depends on one stream of money, such as the income from a job, he is vulnerable should the job be lost. When the Iraqis invaded Kuwait in 1990, the Kuwait government still earned revenue from all its offshore state-owned investments, even

43

though no money was made from oil sales. The principle is the same on a personal level.

If you want to make more money, there are really only two choices: to increase the amount of income you already receive from sources you have already established, such as a job or a business, and to find new sources of income. The Kuwaitis excel at both.

The weakest option of the two is trying to make more money out of your job. First of all, a regular job is simply an exchange of time for money. You are paid to be in a certain place for a certain amount of time. Unless bonuses or sales incentives are included, there isn't much you can do to make more money.

As we saw earlier, giving up a government job doesn't make much sense to most Kuwaitis, so instead they find a way to supplement their salaries. Technically, a Kuwaiti government employee can't own a business, which is why most are registered in the names of family members. The government employee must be at his job during the day, which usually starts at 7:30 A.M. and ends at 2:00 P.M., without lunch breaks. The hours change depending on whether it is summer or winter. With these hours, a second business usually must be run in the evening. Kuwait follows a tradition of shutting most businesses from 1:00 or 1:30 until 4:00 or 4:30 P.M. and then staying open until 7:30 or later.

Some large family businesses employ professional management, so the owner can confidently keep his government job. Others have businesses that only really operate when the owner is present at night. And there are thousands in between.

Many Kuwaitis are creative, original thinkers and bring innovative and original ideas to the country. Almost immediately, just word of mouth in the tight-knit Kuwaiti community can ensure that a venture is a success. The owner begins to consider quitting his government job and devoting all his time and energy to what he thinks is his dream ticket. But another force follows quickly behind him. Several people decide that "hey, this idea works, so let's duplicate it." Soon, what was original becomes commonplace. A personal story will illustrate my point.

My father-in-law started the first health club in Kuwait, back in the early 1960s. For years it stood in the same location, and others of more or less quality came along. Since his place was the first, it maintained its lead. Then came the Iraqi invasion. All the equipment was stolen and the club burned out. My father-in-law and his partners decided not to reopen the place, which may have been an excellent idea.

As Kuwait began to rebuild, people looked for ways to make back the money they had lost. I arrived the same year as liberation and saw it happen. In three short years, there were countless health clubs in apartment building basements all over Kuwait. Each tried to top the one before it, until merely starting a small gym would cost a fortune just to be equal in the market.

45

I decided to step into this fray with my own idea. I was teaching martial arts to U.S. and Kuwaiti special forces, so I took the old health club license and planned a full-time martial arts institute. There were none at the time, except individual classes taught in health clubs and sports clubs. Nobody really believed I could make the idea work, but it has become very successful.

The interesting thing is that the idea proved very difficult to duplicate, since martial arts is a business that revolves around the instructor, instead of mass-marketing floor space in a health club. To date, only one other place has tried to copy the idea of a martial arts school, because of the lack of quality teachers and the economics of the business in Kuwait. However, taking a lesson from the Kuwaitis, I have ventured into other areas, completely unrelated to my martial arts school.

The main principle to be understood is the idea of diversifying your wealth-building efforts to account for risk. Developing many different sources of income is an excellent means of doing that. In the old days of Kuwait, especially during the era of ship building and pearl diving, families began the season with incredible debt. The ship owners would finance fleets of pearl divers. The ship captains would hire crews who needed to leave money for their families so they could live for the many months the men would be at sea. Since this money was borrowed from the fleet owners and captains as advances against the proceeds of the trip, crew members might possibly just break even at the end of the long voyage. Most accumulated large debts.

Waffa Al-Rushaid, director of public relations for the Kuwait Stock Exchange (and, as a matter of clarity, my wife's cousin) points out that this left the women who stayed behind in charge of the family finances.

"The women became very skilled at finding ways to make extra money. They would make bread to sell or whatever they could to stretch their money. This tradition of the women managing the money continues today, and now 60 percent of our customers at the stock exchange are women who manage their own inheritance portfolio."

Such debt-laden living was not the case for the ship owners, who would end the fishing and diving season and then move on to using the ships for international trade. More than a few families became wealthy by smuggling gold to India on such ships. Or they would load their vessels with dates from farms in Iraq and then trade the dates for something in another country, bringing the goods from that place back to Kuwait.

Developing several different sources of income appeals to the traditional merchant mentality of Kuwait and results in many different vertical businesses. It is very common to find a family business that owns, for example, the paint factory, the brush company, the paint can factory, and a venture that employs a large crew of painters.

Many Kuwaiti fortunes had humble beginnings, such as trading, owning shops in the market, financing fishing and pearl-diving expeditions, and owning fleets of boats.

Others diversify into a wide range of unrelated industries and ventures. In the days after the discovery of oil, Kuwait was a country that needed everything for growth, which in turn opened tremendous opportunities. One of the favorite things to do was collect exclusive agencies for products to be sold in the Kuwaiti market. With so much oil wealth flowing, Kuwaiti families could afford to buy many things for their new homes. The government itself needed to create a modern infrastructure for the country, which required buying imported materials and goods. The result was a rush to collect agencies.

A book written about the major merchant families of Kuwait shows this tactic taken to the extreme. Page after page under different family names shows countless well-known brand names, which led to considerable family wealth. Some had so many agencies that eventually their interests went in too many directions and couldn't be properly managed. Others found they didn't have the means or family contacts and networks to develop what agencies they had.

A good example is an acquaintance of mine whose father came to Kuwait from Iran just after the discovery of oil. His father was a man who believed in self-education, and he taught himself, among other languages, English and Japanese. When he began traveling to Japan to bring back products for selling, he eventually was able to win the agency for a major motorcycle manufacturer and a famous electronics

Even today most products have to be imported.

company. He worked hard to develop these agencies, but without the contacts and networks provided by being a member of a large Kuwaiti family, he eventually lost the agencies. The lesson is simple: no matter what business deals you can do, large or small, you have to be able to carry out what the business requires.

For the purpose of our examination of Kuwaiti wealth-building principles, we should remember that Kuwaitis have not done anything different from entrepreneurs in countless other countries do. What changes are the individual opportunities offered by specific circumstances, geographic location, and cultural traditions.

Oil wealth has certainly influenced the character of Kuwait, but the tiny country already had developed a merchant identity. Traditionally, Kuwaiti children (usually sons but sometimes daughters) learn the businesses from their fathers and one day inherit them, often running the ventures very similarly to the way they have been taught.

One of my friends now runs his family's textile business with his brother. They speak with pride of the fact that the business has existed for more than 120 years. If pressed, they can count off and explain very specific lessons passed on by their father, grandfather, and uncle—e.g., always be honest, always give a good deal, always try do business with your brother as a partner.

THE GROWTH OF A FAMILY BUSINESS

(I originally wrote this section as an unpublished article for Kuwait Plus *magazine, and later it was made into a corporate film for Al-Mulla Group.)*

Kuwait in the 1930s was an undeveloped emirate. The traditional pearl industry was suffering from the development of the cultured pearl, and all hopes were on the possibility of oil being discovered.

In 1938, the same year oil was recovered from the Burgan oil field, two men—Saleh Jamal and Abdullah

Saleh Al-Mulla, who was then the government's secretary of state—formed a partnership. They set up a small electrical and domestic appliance shop in the heart of old Kuwait City. Trading under the name Saleh Jamal and Company, the two-man enterprise prospered and soon acquired the agency franchise for a major British electrical company.

By 1947, as Kuwait began to develop its resources, an associate company was founded: The Bader Al-Mulla and Brothers Company. Within a short time, the new enterprise took on the distributorship of Chrysler automobiles and then developed business interests in marine, air-conditioning, travel, equipment supply, and other product lines.

"From 1938 until 1990, our company achieved a steady rate of business growth, not only in sales volume, but in the number of our employees," says Anwar Al-Mulla, deputy chairman of the Al-Mulla Group. "Then came the invasion."

The Al-Mulla Group offices and showrooms were particularly brutalized. What could not be looted was burned and destroyed. After liberation, Al-Mulla Group, like most other companies, was merely an empty shell, without a product to sell or offices to sell it from.

During this post-liberation crisis, the major strength of the Al-Mulla Group became readily apparent: employee loyalty. "Before the invasion, we employed about 3,000 people," Al-Mulla recalls. "After liberation, we were left with only 73, since the others had left the country."

The Al-Mulla family and the employees set to work and were startled to discover that most of the employees were contacting them to come back from abroad. Since the company was in a time of extreme crisis, Al-Mulla could only offer them half-salary, and to everyone's surprise, they accepted.

"We brought everyone back at half-salary and then some months later, three-quarters salary," Al-Mulla remembers. "Finally we were able to pay everyone a full salary, while making up all back wages." The willingness to support the employees, including an all-inclusive incentive plan from the used-car washers to the top management has enabled Al-Mulla to now employ more than 4,300 people.

The two hallmarks of the Al-Mulla business philosophy are unparalleled customer service and professional management designed to support the service.

"Our group is run by a director's committee consisting of 11 people,"

Al-Mulla says. "Four of the directors are Kuwaiti shareholders, and the remainder are expatriates. It is a one-man, one-vote committee, run by a team of professionals."

The range of products and services now offered by the Al-Mulla Group is extensive, including Chrysler, Dodge, and Mitsubishi cars and commercial vehicles, including parts and accessories; Gulf oil products; project engineering; heating, ventilation, and air-conditioning services; transport refrigeration; mechanical and electrical services; building automation and controls; consumer products; domestic and electronic appliances; construction and office equipment; steel fabrication; retail finance; leasing of vehicles and equipment; call taxi services; cleaning, maintenance, and repair services; security services; solid-waste disposal and environmental systems; travel; air freight; fire-fighting equipment; club and entertainment services; advertising; insurance; and consultancy.

Even with such a far-reaching list of products and services, Al-Mulla Group works to keep customer service as the primary management objective, according to Al-Mulla. "We always welcome healthy competition, which provides the customers a good product with good service, at the right price. We do not and will not sacrifice quality of service on account of cost."

Al-Mulla doesn't hesitate when asked to explain the best strength of the Al-Mulla Group. "Our strength is our employees, our principles, and customers. We are always fair to our employees—our biggest asset. Our relationship with our customers is very important to us. We try hard to provide excellent service to attain the best customer satisfaction. It works. Some of our customers have been with us for 56 years."

SMALL BUSINESS IN KUWAIT

The Kuwaitis—and Andrew Carnegie, one of America's richest men—knew that the secret to growing real wealth starts with having your own business. One of the problems in Kuwait, however, is that the local market is so small. The best possible solution is to have income coming from many different product and service lines.

Kuwait does have one certain advantage: low labor costs. Because the cost of imported labor is so inexpensive in Kuwait, many can afford to set up basically absentee-owner businesses. As Carnegie pointed out, "I'd rather have 10 percent of the efforts of 100 men, then 100 percent from one person."

The result of inexpensive labor has been saturation by smaller business with just a few workers. There are entire sections of Kuwait with tiny shop after shop staffed by Indian automobile mechanics or Sri Lankan clothing cleaners or Iranian bakers. The shops often don't make much money, but by Kuwaiti thinking, if you can have a business that makes even just a little money, the business can often pay off later when it is sold.

The buying and selling of small businesses in Kuwait is relatively unsophisticated by U.S. standards. There are too many people trying to compete in a limited market. Those who are not well financed face the hardest challenge. They look around for a business to buy, but because their capital is limited, they often make ill-conceived choices.

The market of Kuwait itself is very small. Recent events have closed the once lucrative markets of Iran and Iraq, so Kuwait often cannot support more than one of certain kinds of factories. Much of the business action ends up taking place on a smaller level. But even on the smallest level, failure to diversify risk can have serious consequences.

As an example, many small commercial fishermen like to catch a fish called *zabaidi*, which is very popular in Kuwait. Recently, however, the Kuwait Institute of Scientific Research advised the government that the zabaidi population needed to be replenished, so, literally overnight, a ban on catching zabaidi was issued for a month. The immediate

Kuwaitis have built wealth by securing agencies for such U.S. companies as 7-Up and Holiday Inn.

result was that too many fishermen tried to sell other types of fish, prices started to drop, and considerable money was lost.

Another favorite Kuwaiti method of dealing with risk is the shared or joint venture. Basically, the concept is the same as in any other country, but in Kuwait, where tax issues aren't a problem, more people get involved. In a later chapter, I will discuss the importance of reputation when doing business in Kuwait; briefly, because of a person's reputation for honesty or other factors, he is invited to join an investment pool.

The members of the investment group may have a very specific project in mind. Someone gets the idea to bring a U.S. franchise to Kuwait, so several people put up money, which buys them a percentage. It's not uncommon for 10, 20, or even more to be involved in such business ventures. The risk and the rewards are spread, since such ventures allow a person to become involved in far more deals than just sinking all his capital in one risky possibility.

INSIDE THE GOLD MARKET

Many Kuwaiti fortunes quietly started, or were significantly built, by smuggling gold to India. Gold has always been a popular commodity in the Middle East because of its value and beauty, and there have always been ready markets for its sale.

During the early decades of the 20th century, smugglers would make their way by sea and land routes to India, carrying gold bullion that, if it survived the journey and didn't fall prey to pirates and bandits, almost certainly would earn handsome profits. When the world price of gold climbed during the 1970s, the precious metal suddenly became too expensive for many of its previous customers.

Kuwait shared in the agonies of gold's rising and falling prices. One who remembers is Ammer, who has been in Kuwait's gold market for the past 20 years. Ammer followed his Syrian father and grandfather in the trade, learning the perils and pleasures of gold from an early age.

"There isn't much of a precious stone or pearl market in Kuwait," Ammer says. "People seem to prefer plain gold. Kuwait is different than many places, because here people like to spend much more money on gold and buy big pieces. They don't mind spending 1,000 KD for a necklace, but in the States or Europe, that would be rare."

One reason for the popularity of gold in Kuwait, according to Ammer, is the relative freedom from crime. "People feel safe here

walking with gold. You can wear a watch cost-
ing 10,000 KD (U.S.$33,000) here without fear
of it being stolen, but somewhere else, you'd
worry about someone cutting off your arm."

A safe society only adds to the appeal of
gold, which in Kuwait has produced a com-
plete market of gold retailers, wholesalers,
and manufacturers.

"Wholesalers here in Kuwait usually buy
the gold from Zurich, Switzerland, and then
ship it to Italy or Singapore or Turkey, where
the manufacturing labor is cheap but of good
quality," he says. "Then they bring it here and
sell it for a profit of 3 to a maximum of 5 percent to the retailers. Then the retailers usually
sell the gold for 15 to 20 percent profit."

Ammer points out for the benefit of potential gold buyers that the wholesalers stick fairly close to quoted gold prices, while the retailers add big markups for the handcrafting
charges. The retail shops compete on the basis
of selection, better salesman, and willingness
to lower profits by lowering prices.

The gold *souk* (market) is the one place,
perhaps better than anywhere else in Kuwait,
where it is very difficult to be cheated if
you're willing to spend time shopping around.
Kuwait offers only four purities of gold,
expressed in karats: 18, 21, 22, and 24, which
is pure gold.

"Here it's hard for a merchant to cheat
someone on the type of gold," Ammer says. "If
the salesman says it's 18 karat, then it's 18,
because the government controls it very strictly.

The stamp that you see on the gold is put there by the government. What a buyer should do is check many shops for a particular piece that you like and ask what the gram price is including handcrafting charges. Some smart salesman might say 3 KD per gram, but when you figure it out, it's actually 5 KD. If you ask, he will say, '3 KD for gold and 2 KD for the handcrafting charge.'"

The gold merchants in Kuwait generally agree that their best customers are the Bedouins, who buy large quantities of gold, both for personal use and to give as marriage dowries.

"Foreigners, like Americans and Europeans, seem to prefer 18 karat, but the Arabs like 21 karat because it is purer, and the Bedouins want 22 karat," Ammer observes. "The craftsmen here have their own special designs, which work well with the tastes of the people in Kuwait, which is why they get many orders. The gold manufacturers in Kuwait work by special order. If you want a design, take it to a manufacturer who will then quote a price which includes the gold and the handcrafting."

Like most other businesses in Kuwait, the dazzling beauty of the gold souk was a special target during the Iraqi invasion. Some shop owners were lucky enough to go immediately to their shops and get the gold out before the soldiers got there. Even during the occupation, solitary soldiers standing watch could be bribed to let some retrieve their merchandise, while others were prevented by the large numbers of soldiers occupying complexes like Al-Muthana. Most gold merchants, including Ammer, lost everything.

"I had my own gold shop in Farwaniya, but the Iraqis took it all. I was in the United States then, so I could do nothing. Now I work for someone else until I can save enough money to start another business of my own."

Ammer, like many other merchants and customers, prefers gold over other commodities. "I like the gold business because it's so simple," he says. "Gold is something you can carry with you, which is why many people who survived the invasion think that gold is better than cash."

Another side effect of the invasion came after liberation, when many of the former heavy buyers of gold were not permitted back into the country. "The market has gone down since the invasion because the people who buy more gold than other foreigners, the Palestinians and the Iraqis, didn't come back into the country."

One indication of gold's popularity is the number of gold shops. There are nearly 1,500 in Kuwait, and most big areas have a special section just for the gold shops.

CHAPTER FOUR

The Kuwaiti Stock Market

Wall Street is the only place that people ride to in a Rolls Royce to take advice from those who took the subway.

—Warren Buffett

Waffa Al-Rushaid, public relations director for the Kuwait Stock Exchange, likes to show visitors the stock certificate framed on her wall. A large piece of paper with a picture of a sailing ship, the share certificate is more than 150 years old.

"This certificate shows that a Kuwaiti man purchased 15,000 shares of the Arab Shipping Company for 12,500 Indian rupees," says Al-Rushaid. "It also means that Kuwaitis have been dealing with shares for a very long time."

The eagerness of the Kuwaiti investor to invest in stock shares is partially the result of a small, limited investment market. Traditional means of employing capital, such as investing in business and industry, are severely limited by the small market size of Kuwait. Often the country can only support one or no more than two factories in a particular industry, simply because there are not enough people in Kuwait to buy the product. The result: investing in shares of companies that already exist.

THE ORIGINS OF THE STOCK MARKET

The early version of the stock market started just after the first shareholder company, the National Bank of Kuwait, was formed in 1952. The trading of shares was very informal. People who were well connected in Kuwait would act as middlemen, putting buyers and sellers together and taking a commission. When the number of people involved started growing, the Ministry of Commerce set up a small department to oversee the trading. According to Al-Rushaid, the first 20 years were plagued with a serious problem: the amount of money necessary to deal in the stock market.

"The major problem was the high price of the shares, which were as high as 100 to 200 KD per share [U.S.$330 to $660 at today's exchange rates]," says Al-Rushaid. "You couldn't buy small amounts either. You could only buy in lots of 5,000 or 10,000 shares, large numbers like that. This meant that only the best companies were being traded, and only the very wealthy were involved in the buying and selling."

Because of the small market size, the Kuwait Stock Exchange doesn't have the same harried craziness of the U.S. stock markets.

In the early 1970s, events started to unfold that changed Kuwait's stock market activities. As the price of oil continued to rise, Kuwaitis found themselves with more money to spend. The war between Egypt and Israel in 1973 laid the foundation for what would become Kuwait's major stock crisis.

THE SOUK AL-MANAKH CRISIS

The first major impact of the 1973 Arab-Israeli War was an oil embargo, which in turn created higher oil prices. Virtually overnight, the Kuwaitis found themselves flush with money and no place to invest it, especially small investors.

At the time, there was no law preventing the trading of company shares outside the formal stock market, overseen by the Ministry of Commerce. Many small companies were economically viable, but their size prevented them from being listed on the main exchange. In much the same way as the earlier version of the official stock market, a second alternative developed.

Souk Al-Manakh (roughly pronounced al-ma-knock) referred to a specific building called the Manakh complex, which housed many real estate offices. Businessmen gathered there and eventually began trading in small-company shares.

This shadow market developed quickly. The main method of deal making became forward trading, which meant that a buyer would go to a seller and make a deal with a postdated check. The trade might be for a certain amount of shares at a total price of 10,000 KD, but if the seller would wait for payment for six months, for example, the buyer would pay him a 1,000 KD premium. This represented an additional 10 percent for doing nothing more than waiting. These extra payments went as high as 500 percent.

The entire system was based on the trust that nobody would cash the postdated checks early, even though legally they could. As thousands of Kuwaitis took part, share prices

Kuwaitis diversify risk, especially after the Al-Manakh crash, by keeping assets in Kuwait banks and investing abroad.

reached ridiculously high levels, without any regard for the company's financial fundamentals. Many companies existed only on paper. Small shops used as the licensed headquarters for companies were trading for $1,000,000 and more. According to Al-Rushaid and others, billions of dollars changed hands inside Kuwait during these years.

Circumstances started to create an even more unstable situation as the Iran-Iraq War continued in 1982. In August of that same year, someone tried to cash the postdated check of one of Kuwait's wealthiest people—

69

and it bounced. Mob psychology took over as people panicked and started trying to cash checks only to find that most were bad. The man whose check bounced was responsible for nearly half of the bad debt.[1]

According to Al-Rushaid, the crisis touched all aspects of Kuwaiti society and has taken 15 years to resolve. The end result, however, was a highly regulated stock market, which has become one of the most successful in the Middle East.

Today, smaller investors can take part in the stock market, but the stakes are still high. According to Al-Rushaid, minimum blocks of shares still cost 4,000 to 5,000 KD (U.S.$13,200 to 16,500).

"The small investors, the ones who invest 10,000 or 20,000 KD, are the ones who tend to panic when the stock prices drop," says Al-Rushaid. "They often have a large part of their portfolio tied up with us and can't afford to be patient during downturns. So they start selling and prices drop."

The stock market—in Kuwait and elsewhere—depends on what the investors think is happening in the market as much as what actually does occur. This was especially evident on "Black Monday," October 19, 1987, when the Dow-Jones Industrial Average suffered its largest loss since the Great Crash of 1929. Kuwait is not linked to the New York Stock Exchange or any other in the United States, but still the 1987 crash was felt in Kuwait City: the Kuwait Stock Exchange suffered a 30 percent drop. According to Al-Rushaid, there were three basic reasons.

"The first was psychological," remembers Al-Rushaid. "This happened only five years after Al-Manakh, so people were scared that the same thing was going to happen again. The second reason was that the investment sector companies listed on our exchange had large parts of their portfolios overseas. The third reason was that individual investors had North American portfolios, and when these dropped, many had to sell shares from their Kuwait portfolios to cover the losses."

LESSONS FOR WEALTH BUILDING

This book does not discuss specific investment techniques for stocks, bonds, and mutual funds. Any trip to a large bookstore will prove that the last thing the world needs is another book for small investors. But there are some important lessons to be learned from the Kuwaitis' experiences with buying and selling stock.

The first, and probably most important, lesson is not to think that tomorrow's market returns will be as successful as today's. One thing that fueled the speculation in the Al-Manakh crisis was simple greed. But a second was the belief that the good times would last forever or, at the very least, a little longer.

Several people who took part in the Al-Manakh trading privately admit that they were caught up in the numbers. So much money was being traded that many chose to ignore the potential downside. There were some prudent investors who jumped in, made some cash, and got out again. Most didn't; hence the 15 years needed for Kuwait to resolve the effects of the crisis.

The second lesson is critical: investors who fail to diversify will also fail to make money in the long run. Many of the investors who entered the shadow stock market used most of the spare cash they could find. When the house of cards collapsed, they were finished. Smart investors in Kuwait not only invest in different sectors inside Kuwait, but they also keep a large share of their portfolios outside the country.

Lesson three: companies that exist only on paper aren't worth the paper that gives them life. In an *Arab Times* article dated April 30, 1997, the director-general of the Kuwait Stock Exchange, Hisham Al-Oteibi, suggested that both large and small investors should "be educated and read the financial data which we [the Stock Exchange] and the listed firms issue and base decisions accordingly, not following speculators."

He made these remarks after two days of record trading on the Kuwait Stock Exchange, which some were suggesting didn't correspond with company financial reports, but instead with investor emotion. At the time of this writing, some critics are giving the same warnings about the U.S. markets as well. The point is clear: smart investors should pay attention to the fundamentals of making money in stocks, bonds, and mutual funds. Leave the gun-slinging emotional speculation to the investors who can afford to lose. Traditionally, stock shares have offered one of the best ways to build one's wealth, but it can't be done without an education. You must learn how stock investing works, whether you are buying individual shares or mutual funds. As the Kuwaitis learned, the price of just jumping in without considering the consequences can take years to repay.

NOTE

1. Jill Crystal, *Oil and Politics in the Gulf: Rulers and Merchants in Kuwait and Qatar* (Cambridge, UK: Cambridge University Press, 1995).

CHAPTER FIVE

The Value of Owning Land

Most people have five senses: sight, smell, taste, touch, and hearing. The successful have two more: horse and common. [However] this is an age in which we cannot find common sense without a search warrant.

—George F. Will

Land has always been a valuable asset, no matter in what country. *Forbes* magazine reported that 28 of the 400 richest Americans built their wealth with real estate. Physically, land has the advantages of being a fixed quantity, subject to supply and demand; it is permanent; it is improvable. But real estate also has several more distinct advantages for building wealth.

LAND'S BIGGEST
WEALTH-BUILDING SECRETS

1. *Wealth is increased by leveraging land.* You can take ownership with only a small amount of your own money up front. Bill Fitzpatrick, a well-known business writer (www.success.org), makes a clear case for the leverage advantages of real estate:

    > An investor has $20,000. If he puts the entire amount in a stock investment and makes $4,000, he has a 20 percent return. Most would say that he made a great stock investment. If that same investor used the $20,000 as a down payment on a $100,000 apartment building and the building appreciated just 4 percent, he'd have a 20 percent return. However, the real estate investor would also have a sizable tax shelter return and perhaps an additional return from cash flow. And, eventually, the rents will pay off the mortgage.

    Kuwait offered a unique twist on this advantage, which came as a direct result of the Iraqi invasion. After the liberation of Kuwait, the government decided to absorb consumer installment loans made before the invasion. This meant that many people, some of whom had only recently taken a mortgage when the invasion occurred, had their mortgages paid off.

2. *Wealth is increased by cash flow.* When you own land, you can rent it for more than the mortgage payment owed and other expenses incurred. This surplus goes toward building wealth.

3. *Wealth is increased because of property's appreciation.* The real estate's value can increase as a result of inflation or improvements to the property.

4. *Wealth is increased as the mortgage is paid off.* Each time you make a mortgage payment, part of the money goes toward the repayment of principal. This increases your net worth by increasing the amount of equity in the property.

5. *Wealth is increased because of tax benefits.* In the United States, for example, a property owner has such tax advantages as mortgage interest deductions, property tax payment deductions, and allowances for property depreciation.

6. *Wealth is increased by one's reputation as a property owner.* Kuwaiti perceptions often give advantages to individuals and families who are perceived as large property owners.

The beginning of Kuwait the country was Kuwait the town, which was surrounded by the sea on one side and the protective wall on the other.

THE BEGINNING OF LAND WEALTH IN KUWAIT

The tiny amount of land available in Kuwait has played a central role in the accumulation of wealth by its citizens. In the late 18th century, Kuwait was only a tiny seafront community. To protect themselves, the citizens built a huge wall around the town, with only a few gates for entry. The wall especially protected the city when the majority of the males were off at sea, either diving for pearls or trading in some foreign country.

When the oil income started in 1946–47, Kuwait's rulers decided to spread the wealth among their citizens. One of the face-saving ways they used centered around land; their first method was to encourage people to take plots outside the city walls. The government would then buy the person's property inside the city walls for extremely generous amounts. Large wealthy families who owned lots of land not only made serious amounts of money by selling property inside the city walls, they also acquired large tracts of land outside the walls, which would later be sold for substantial profits. **79**

When oil was developed, the Kuwait government bought property inside the city and encouraged the Kuwaiti citizens to buy or claim land beyond the safety of the city gates.

FIXED QUANTITIES

Kuwait is a small country, approximately 6,880 square miles or slightly larger than Connecticut. Much of the land, however, is not available for habitation because it covers oil reserves. The majority of the country's residents live in an area that radiates from the original town on Kuwait Bay. By habit or choice, the large Kuwaiti families have concentrated their lives in relatively small areas and now are unwilling to go much farther away.

Today prime real estate in Kuwait is very limited and in high demand.

These facts have both created an incredible demand for residential property within these areas and raised the price of land to increasingly higher levels. Some reports note that residential land in Kuwait costs as much as any land in the world, including New York City and Tokyo. The point is not that there is a shortage of land in Kuwait, but rather a shortage of land where people are willing to live or where the infrastructure for building has been developed.

If the United States offered its citizens an interest-free housing loan of $200,000, the odds are high that there would be an abundance of homes for sale at the amazing price of $195,000. You could close the deal with money in your pocket. But in Kuwait, since the demand for residential land is so high, the 70,000 KD offered by the government may just cover the cost of the land and not the construction of the house itself. The high cost of buying property and building a house keeps prices so high that many can't afford to buy, even with the huge (by U.S. standards) interest-free loan.

LAND IS IMPROVABLE

In terms of wealth building, owning land has always had the advantage of being improvable. You can make money by renting the property. You can use the land as collateral to take out a loan for another business venture. You could use the land as part of a deal where someone builds a factory on your property and gives you an interest in it.

DISADVANTAGES TO OWNING LAND

Of course, there are few disadvantages to owning land: you have to pay property taxes in the United States, and the land often can be devalued by circumstances you can't control. In some areas in the United States, there has been an overabundance of developed office space and apartments, causing real estate prices to nose-dive.

After the war in Kuwait, a similar set of

circumstances started to develop. People who owned land started building six- and eight-unit apartment blocks on their property, with the justification that they could get more income than simply building a large villa and renting it to one tenant. But during the 1970s and 1980s, there had been a building boom in apartment complexes, mostly occupied by expatriate nationalities.

Thousands of people did not return to the country after liberation. This situation created a surplus of empty apartments, but the building of new ones went merrily on. Some areas of Kuwait now have multiple units with high rents and bad parking because the original intention was to have single-family dwellings.

THE CONCEPT OF KEY MONEY

The overabundance of available commercial space in the United States allows a potential lessor to demand negotiating levers like several months' free rent, rebates on maintenance fees, and other concessions. In Kuwait, however, good commercial locations are extremely limited, which drives up rent and allows owners or lease holders to ask for *key money*.

Key money simply means that a person who wants a particular space would have to pay for the right to rent it. For example, one of the prime commercial areas in Kuwait is an area called Salmiya, and in that area are sub-areas where new construction is taking place. One such area has many U.S. franchise

Considerable fortunes have been made by developing Kuwait's real estate, as is illustrated by the following photographs.

85

restaurants and other features that draw customers. The shops in these areas can ask for and receive $50,000 and more for the right to take the lease. This means that a person planning a business must build into his business not only the costs of starting and growing his venture, but also this large up-front cost. The requirement of paying key money is often the reason that a person who would have normally started a sole proprietorship has no choice but to find partners.

A REPUTATION AS A LANDOWNER

Many cultures give special status to "a man of property." This benefit is especially valuable in Kuwait, where owning land can often give a person a higher degree of respectability. Owning land in Kuwait is rarely a bad investment, so conversation among Kuwaiti men often centers on the latest clever real estate deal.

Because the family plays such a crucial role in Kuwaiti society, relatives will join together to buy real estate, forming companies with family members as partners. These holding companies are usually given the family name, for example, the Abdul Smith and Sons Real Estate Development Company. Buying and holding real estate is only one of the goals of the business. The other is improving the family's status in Kuwait. The importance and business value of a good reputation will be discussed at length in Chapter 6.

AN AMERICAN EXAMPLE OF THE KUWAITI APPROACH TO REAL ESTATE

Matt Young, columnist and contributing editor for *Overseas Digest*, works from his farm in Lancaster, Ohio. He and his wife, Michele, offer an excellent example of how to apply the Kuwaiti approach to wealth building through real estate. He explains:

Michele and I wanted to own our farm before we were 26. We missed our date by two months, but that wasn't so bad. The farm was 110 acres of rolling hills, 20 acres or so wooded, a rundown old house, and a couple barns that were falling down.

Michele and I had looked at other farms before this one, but we were having trouble finding financing. There were government loan programs, but you really had to be a farmer already. We quickly realized that we were going to have to have financing from the seller. We talked to a few real estate brokers, but none of them wanted to find us a farm that was seller-financed.

Michele found the farm in a small classified advertising newspaper. It was the only time and place the owners ever advertised it. The asking price was $80,000. The owners wanted $20,000 down and the rest of the money on a three-year land contract. They offered an 11 percent interest rate. Today that interest rate seems high, but this was 1986, and many farms overborrowed on inflated land prices. When the price of corn collapsed so did many farmers. This was why we were not able to find financing on our own.

Our credit was spotless, and we had used a lot of credit over the past five years. We did not have the

$20,000, so we offered $5,000 down payment and an 11.5 interest rate. The owners accepted the new interest rate but not the down payment. They counteroffered a $10,000 down payment. The payment was amortized over 30 years, even though the contract was for only three years. We also negotiated a three-year extension of the payments if we made all of the payments for the first three years on time.

We hired a lawyer to draw up the land contract. The sellers' lawyer also wanted to draw up a contract, but ours was done first. We haggled over a couple of details, such as possession.

For the first two years we rented to a farmer for $50 per acre, for 71 tillable acres. He planted it in corn and put the rest in a government subsidy program.

Because of his research about the past planting history, we were able to enter the 71 acres into a government program that is designed to protect highly erodible soil. The program was the Conservation Reserve Program (CRP), a 10-year program that is done by bidding. I bid to the government how much I want for my acreage. Because mine was the target soil type, I bid above the average, the average being about $50 per acre. I bid $84.50. The bid was accepted, and we signed a 10-year contract to leave the ground in cover crop (clover, orchard grass, and timothy).

Our current payment from the government is $5,670 per year. We did have setup costs to join the program and had to add soil nutrients, lime, and fertilizers. This amounted to about half of the first year's payment. Over 10 years, we will earn $56,700.50 from this program. You can also consider that periodic sale of some of the farm's timber has given about $10,000 dollars. With the payments from the government and the sale of timber, 90 percent of the original land contract will be covered.

We have since built a new house on the property, and we often get offers to subdivide our land and sell off as smaller parcels. If I could get a regional zoning variance (which I probably could), I could subdivide the frontage approximately 10 times, selling nine parcels. If I could not get the variance, I could subdivide off five additional parcels.

The parcels could be large, up to five acres. This is a highly desirable size, worth $30,000 a piece. With a variance, this would equal $270,000; without a variance, $150,000. Keep in mind that there would still be 60 to 80 acres of the farm remaining behind the parcels of land that were subdivided.

I am not interested in this kind of subdivision of the land. It is my belief that the farm will be, in the long run, more valuable as a single tract of land.

There is an added benefit besides numerous federal and state tax savings. We enjoy a reduced property tax because it's a farm. We are also in a county program called the Current Agriculture Use Valuation, [which allows us to pay] only $380 a year in property taxes, which is extremely cheap for where we live.

CHAPTER SIX

Kuwaiti Networking

A miser isn't any fun to live with, but he makes a wonderful ancestor.

—Anonymous

In the vast desert expanses of the Arabian peninsula, where most of the Kuwaiti families originated, one's honesty and integrity formed the backbone of family honor. Centuries of Arab tradition have cemented the idea that the family name, and family honor, is larger than any one individual member.

Trust was crucial for the families that depended on the sea. During long months at sea, the divers and sailing crews usually needed an advance on their earnings to provide for their families. Those who stayed behind helped each other through emergencies and lean times. Giving a willing hand to the others in the community went far in adding honor to the family.

Anything can have an effect on the family name. Even today in the Middle East, you can sometimes read in the newspaper about a brother's killing his sister because she did something to shame the family, such as having an adulterous affair. Privately, people will tell you that while they don't agree with murder, they can "understand why the brother did it."

Another of the old Arabic traditions is the idea of repaying a debt of honor. This repayment can sometimes carry over into future generations from the person who incurred the debt. A personal example will make this clearer.

My wife's grandfather started the first magazine in the Persian Gulf during the 1920s. He decided to support the king of Saudi Arabia politically when there were many plots against him. Sometime later, the king sent my wife's grandfather to Indonesia as an Islamic missionary, and he was subsequently murdered there.

To this day, the family of that king accepts a debt of honor to my wife's family for her grandfather's support and sacrifice. One way this debt has been acknowledged and repaid was immediately following the liberation of Kuwait City after the Iraqi invasion.

Only a couple of days after the coalition forces retook Kuwait City, a large white truck pulled up outside my wife's family home in one of the older aristocratic suburbs. The driver said the truck was from the former king's family. When family members opened the back of the cargo truck, they found food, water, an electric generator, cans of fuel, and other scarce commodities needed in the war-torn city.

My wife's family, like so many others, also received help after liberation from extended family members in other countries, including Saudi Arabia. This seems strange by U.S. standards because the "extended family" means several cousins removed, sixth, seventh, or more. Traditionally, the Arabs just refer to them as "our cousins," which means that certain family obligations must be observed.

The wide extended family is often a means of building wealth, simply by having several members of a group working for a common cause: the family's businesses. The extended family is not, however, the only method of networking. Another family tradition used to stay in contact with people is the *diwaniya*.

THE DIWANIYA

Kuwait's hospitality is legendary in the Middle East, and much of this reputation is rooted in the traditional gathering place. The diwaniya, or "little parliament," is a unique meeting place that plays a central role in the social, commercial, and political fabric of the community.

97

Gathering and talking has always been the chief means of communication in Kuwait.

The traditional location of the diwaniya has always been a smaller building outside the host's home, except where it has been specially designed as an area of the house. Even then, the diwaniya is always distinct and some distance away from the main living quarters.

Diwaniyas are as different as their hosts. Some are richly furnished marble buildings owned by influential businessmen for commercial as well as social purposes. Open-air diwaniyas are a frequent sight, either at the front or the rear of a private home. It is not unusual to see groups of 12 or more gathered outside on a large carpet on the cooler Kuwaiti evenings.

The diwaniya can be a tent, a special room, or a building (right) separate from the main house.

But the majority of diwaniyas are held in tents or in specially designed rooms attached to private homes. Many have thick-carpeted floors surrounded by pillows for comfort or soft benches running the length of the diwaniya along three or four walls.

An individual who hosts a diwaniya must make a long-term commitment, and although most are only held one night a week, some are open every evening. By tradition, everyone who enters or attends a diwaniya is welcome. Each time a person enters the diwaniya, he is honored with a standing welcome and introductory handshakes with all present.

99

Kuwaiti diwaniyas are meant for discussion, relaxation, and hospitality.

The diwaniyas are everywhere, in every town and village in Kuwait and on almost every street. It is said that a man could visit a different diwaniya every night of the year. And while the diwaniya has traditionally been a male institution, women's diwaniyas are flourishing, as are mixed diwaniyas in some areas.

These traditional meeting places originated in the ancient culture of the nomadic Bedouin and developed later as a practical means of trade and social communication. Eighteenth century records refer to dockside *ghawas*, or coffeehouses, where international traders, merchants, and vessel owners openly invited

The main ingredients of Arab hospitality include coffee and tea.

returning sailors and traders from other lands to meet with them over dinner to discuss business. That mixture of Kuwaiti openness and a consuming need for information has transformed the diwaniya into an essential part of modern Kuwaiti life and commerce.

Ahmed, a retired Kuwaiti businessman, says the tradition of hosting his family's diwaniya has passed down from his grandfather, a successful merchant, to his father, and now to him. Ahmed now hosts his gathering once a week in a fashionable section of Kuwait City.

"By talking and listening to our parents and grandparents, we have been able to retain our traditions and maintain many of the features which have been part of the Kuwaiti life for hundreds of years," says Ahmed. "This is part of our history and a part of our freedom."

To preserve those traditions and ensure that they are passed on to future generations, boys as young as 10 years old are encouraged to attend diwaniyas to listen to the discussions and learn from their elders. In the past, it was not unusual for the *amirs* of Kuwait (the country's rulers) or members of the ruling family to keep in touch with their subjects by visiting Kuwaitis in their diwaniyas. Today, the diwaniya provides Kuwaitis with opportunities to express their views on any subject, listen to the views of others, and then formally debate issues and opinions.

Sami, a 30-year-old Kuwaiti professional, hosts a diwaniya once a week in a basement room designed to accommodate up to 50 people. His father, Yacoub, spent a lifetime collecting the Persian carpets and tapestries that adorn the spacious room. After Yacoub's retirement, he passed the diwaniya on to Sami, who relishes the prospect of entertaining friends and visitors every Monday night. Yacoub tells stories from the past to a mix of young professionals, friends, and members of the immediate family, while Sami plays host. Yacoub views the role of the diwaniya as a ·est from the pressures of modern life.

"Every year, life gets just a little more com-·ed, and with that comes the increasing · of dealing with those daily rigors,"

A usual topic of discussion in the diwaniya is politics.

says Yacoub. "The diwaniya provides a conve-
nient outlet for friends to meet on a regular
basis and to discuss current events, business,
and community matters. Different diwaniyas
focus on different interests. You will find
diwaniyas which are devoted to finance and
economics, while others are purely political."

There are no topics forbidden for discussion. Every member of the diwaniya is enti-
tled to speak, offer opinions, and participate
fully. It has become the custom for politicians
to float ideas in the diwaniyas and then judge
the reaction of their communities. In the
small country of Kuwait, the diwaniya net-
work has become an efficient means of mass

103

communication, ensuring that public affairs issues and political ideas reach a large segment of the population.

"Our diwaniya is very informal, like most others in Kuwait," says Yacoub. "We meet once a week, talk, play cards, and carry on discussions after dinner."

Yacoub's diwaniya evening ends after midnight, but it is not unusual for members to stay until dawn playing a traditional Kuwaiti card game. Even though gambling is prohibited, the game occasionally provokes an intense but friendly rivalry.

Tradition dictates that any discussions that become too heated during debate must not be carried outside the diwaniya, and any argument must end at the door before anyone leaves.

Kuwait's diwaniyas are unlike social gatherings in the Western world, where friends and acquaintances are usually invited to either a business function or something strictly social, such as a weekend barbecue at someone's home. Among its Arab neighbors, the diwaniya is exclusive to Kuwait and is a proudly maintained tradition symbolizing the warm hospitality that is a fundamental part of Kuwait's culture.

"For us here, my diwaniya is open to anybody," says Yacoub. "If anyone sees the diwaniya, he can come in and have tea, eat dinner with us, and be made welcome. It is part of our tradition, and it is in our blood."

By limiting the frequency to once a week, the host is free to visit other diwaniyas in return. Food may or may not be served, and largely depends on the financial status of the host, since he often must feed large groups of people. Since rice is the staple food of Kuwait, those diwaniyas that do offer meals traditionally serve a *briyani* rice mixture with meat, poultry, or fish.

Although tradition dictates that the guests must be seated on the floor and the meal eaten only by hand, most hosts provide guests with the choice of utensils and some serve dinner at a large table in a separate room. All diwaniyas serve coffee or tea, but alcohol is forbidden.

The majority of diwaniyas are held during the evening, but women tend to hold theirs in the morning or during the day. There are also diwaniyas in the morning for elderly men, who are treated with great respect.

I attend at least two diwaniyas, and they are very different. One diwaniya includes mostly the male members of my mother-in-law's side of the family. We meet on Sunday evenings, and dinner is always served. One of the interesting features of this diwaniya is a custom they started among themselves. Each month, every member pays a small amount of money into a general fund. As this general fund grows, it is used for anything voted for and approved by the members. Generally, the approved purposes are for emergencies incurred by one of the family or when someone needs financial help.

The second diwaniya I attend is hosted by the brother of one of my martial arts students.

The brother manages the private business affairs of the country's prime minister. This diwaniya tends to be larger in size and is held on Friday evenings. At both places, I will hear discussions on a wide range of topics, from business to politics.

The diwaniyas in Kuwait are different from the calculating sort of networking that often takes place in the West, the "honey, I'm joining the country club to win friends and influence people" approach. Although people do talk business at the diwaniya, that is certainly not its main purpose.

Even though new members are treated with respect and hospitality, my experience has been that many people present will be guarded and reserved until they know you much better. Your reputation in Kuwait is what brings the business opportunities, and a reputation takes time to develop. Because of the tremendous amount of discussion that takes place among Kuwaitis, word of a person's reputation, good or bad, can spread very quickly. I've actually been to diwaniyas where I didn't know anyone except the person who took me, but people there will know me as "the American with the martial arts school." This makes the difference between being treated as a stranger and being welcomed as someone familiar.

In Kuwait, your reputation is crucially important for wealth building. If you are known as a good, honest person, who does what he says he will do when he says he will

do it, you can take advantage of many opportunities. This means the same as having a reputation with your banker as a good credit risk,
so if a business opportunity comes your way,
you can get the credit necessary to take it.

Wealth-Building Strategies and Tactics

An archer is not known for his arrows, but for his aim.

—Anonymous

In this chapter, I have distilled some of the major lessons contained in this book. Please use them as a starting point to think about and plan your efforts at wealth building. With today's technology, you can easily find much more information for each point, especially as it pertains to you and your individual circumstances.

Building wealth is as much a matter of education as it is lucky breaks and chance opportunities. As John Jacob Astor pointed out, wealth is largely a matter of habit.

The Kuwaitis' main strategy for the future is to never forget the past.

WEALTH BUILDING MADE EASY

The overall strategy of wealth building that has been explored in this book includes the following four steps:

1. *Start with the money you already have, whether from a job, a business, an inheritance, a windfall, or another income source.*

2. *Spend less money than you make.*
3. *Put the difference to work making more money.*
4. *Protect your assets and your money-making abilities.*

RECOGNIZING OPPORTUNITY

Opportunity always exists if you know where to find it. But to find opportunity and take advantage of it, you need a specific kind of education. You have to assess what you have working for you. You have to know about the way the world works. You have to know how money works.

TAKE CHARGE OF WHAT YOU CAN

You can set goals and work toward them, but you can't control the emergencies and contingencies that will happen along the way. You can't control the future of Social Security or government pensions, but you do have control over the cash you save for your retirement. If you work for someone or some company, you can't control whether you lose your job, but you can control earning other income from additional sources or starting your own business.

You can't control the tax rate, but you can control your tax payments by knowing that you only have to pay the minimum amount required by law. What is that minimum amount for you? You can't control inflation, but you can choose high-quality investments to offset inflation. You can't control rising costs, but you can control how much you spend, and, more important, how much you save. You can also control the risk of your investments, by choice and diversification.

SETTING FINANCIAL GOALS

Ask yourself what you are trying to accomplish with your wealth building. What exact financial goal are you trying to reach? Don't just say, "I want money; I want to be rich." How much are you trying to earn? Write down a specific amount, and then make a few notes about why you have chosen that figure.

FIGURE OUT WHERE
YOU ARE RIGHT NOW

Make a detailed evaluation of where you right now. Determine exactly how much income you have and from what sources. Exactly how much do you spend every month?

What assets do you own and what are they worth? How much to you owe and to whom?

What specific skills, interests, and hobbies, do you have? Try to write down as many things as you can, no matter how trivial they may seem. Think about how these might be used to help reach your wealth-building goals.

NETWORKING

What networks of people do you have access to? Are you a member of a club or association? A large family? A small, familiar community? List them all. Try to identify possible ways they can help your wealth-building plans.

Do you know anyone personally you consider rich? Why do you think he or she is wealthy? Is it the car he or she drives or the house he or she lives in? Have you ever talked to that person about how he or she became wealthy? What can this person teach you?

CONTROLLING WHAT YOU SPEND

You should make a detailed list of what you owe and to whom and a list of what you spend every month. Look at the monthly list in terms of what is necessary and what is not. Are there any areas which you can sacrifice in order to have extra money to put to work for you?

Don't Pay Full Price

Look at all the areas where you spend money, whether it is monthly expenses, or habitual things like buying new clothes, new cars, or whatever. Try to find ways around the paying of full price for these items. You have to educate yourself about each expense category and then seek out alternatives to paying the normal full price. Don't think of it as torture, think of this as a sport called "controlling my money."

Find an expert who can review your major expenses, such as taxes, insurance, home mortgage, and car loans. Have this person determine whether you are paying the lowest possible prices and payments for what you are getting. Would term insurance work better for you than whole life? Can your mortgage be refinanced at a better rate? Are you paying the lowest possible amount of taxes given your circumstances?

Become a Master at Bargaining

Start to practice the fine art of bargaining. One good place to start is going to somewhere small and unintimidating, such as a flea market or a garage sale, and practice. Set it in your mind that you want to bargain until the price is a specific level that you set, like a quarter or a half lower. When you feel confident with smaller circumstances, try it with larger-ticket items.

Educate Yourself about the Money You Spend

Start reading about ways to lower your monthly expenses by subscribing to newsletters or magazines covering such topics. The idea is not necessarily to reduce yourself to eating macaroni and cheese out of a box, but to educate yourself about how variable the prices you pay actually are.

Pay Yourself First

Follow the ancient wisdom of "paying yourself first." Having money working for you begins with treating savings as an expense that must be paid. Take a small amount and put it aside first as savings and watch how easy it is to adjust. Automatic payroll deduction plans are a good way to accomplish this. You can't spend what you don't see.

Reevaluate Your Credit Cards

Take a long hard look at your credit cards. Do you have too many? Can you get by without most of them? Try alternatives such as a secured card, with which you can't charge beyond the limit of the money you have on deposit.

Don't Buy a New Car

As soon as you drive a new car off the lot, depreciation begins, and the interest charges continue to eat away at your money. By spending your money on a used car, even one that is two years old, you save significantly because so much depreciation has already occurred.

STRATEGIES FOR PUTTING YOUR EXCESS MONEY TO WORK

1. *Understand that any strategy you attempt for investing your available money must account for risk.* How much risk can you accept? What strategies have you employed to offset some of the risk?
2. *Look into starting a small business without drastically changing your present circumstances.* From the Kuwaiti perspective, this could be something as simple as finding

something you can buy at one price and then resell it for a profit. Your goal is to learn the mechanics and principles of doing business so that you can eventually build up to a bigger, more profitable situation.

3. *Make sure that you have protected your assets and yourself with the proper levels of insurance.* This includes a liquid emergency cash fund. Money for growing wealth may be tied up for some time, so you should be prepared for emergencies in such fashion that you don't have to touch your extra capital.

4. *Investigate business ventures where you can have others working for you, not as employees, but as income generators.* Today, these types of opportunities would include what is called multilevel marketing (MLM). The key word here is *investigate*. MLM businesses are plagued with scam artists, so do your homework. Keep in mind that from a Kuwaiti perspective, the ability to earn money from your "downline" is risky if the MLM structure is built around the sale of a single product or service. If anything happens to that product or service that prevents its sale, then you lose big.

5. *Remember that often when you start a new business, momentum picks up quickly, and you are left with something far bigger than you are prepared to manage.* In your desire to build wealth, take it a step at a time. Don't count on the overnight route to wealth and prosperity.

6. *Investigate the idea of buying into a venture with a group of people you know and trust.* The risks are very high, simply because so many personalities will be involved, but often this is a good way to build wealth. As "Fast Eddie" Felson said in the film *The Hustler,* "A small piece of something big is better than 100 percent of nothin'."

7. *Constantly watch the figures and observations you make (see "Controlling What You Spend," above).* If you start having a little success generating extra cash, don't be in a hurry to spend it. Keep your financial goals in mind. Don't let life-style changes eat away at your wealth before you have a chance to build it.

Stocks and Mutual Funds

Traditionally, stock shares have offered one of the best ways to build one's wealth, but it can't be done without an education. You must learn how stock investing works, whether you are buying individual shares or mutual funds. The price of jumping in without considering the consequences can take years to repay. To be successful in the stock market, observe these three lessons:

1. *Do not think that tomorrow's market returns will be as successful as today's.* Don't believe the good times will last forever. This is probably the most important lesson of all.

2. *Investors who fail to diversify will also fail to make money in the long run.* This lesson is critical to learn and practice.
3. *Smart investors should pay strict attention to the fundamentals of making money in stocks, bonds, and mutual funds.* Leave the gun-slinging emotional speculation to the investors who can afford to lose.

Six Good Reasons to Invest in Real Estate

1. *Your wealth is increased by cash flow.* When you own land, you can rent it for more than the mortgage payment owed and other expenses incurred. This surplus goes toward building wealth.
2. *Your wealth is increased because of property's appreciation.* The value of real estate can increase as a result of inflation or improvements made to the property.
3. *Your wealth is increased as the mortgage is paid off.* Each time you make a mortgage payment, part of the money goes toward the repayment of principal. This increases your net worth by increasing the amount of equity in the property.
4. *Your wealth is increased because of tax benefits.* In the United States, for example, a property owner has such tax advantages as mortgage interest deductions, property tax payment deductions, and allowances for property depreciation.
5. *Your wealth may increase through your reputation as a landowner.* Advantages are often

119

gained by individuals who are perceived as large property owners.

6. *Your wealth is increased because you can take ownership with only a small amount of your own money up front.*

THE VALUE OF A GOOD REPUTATION

Your reputation is crucially important for building wealth. A good reputation can bring business opportunities, but it takes time to develop. If you are known as a good, honest person, who does what he says he will, when he says he will do it, you are often able to take advantage of unexpected opportunities. This means the same as having a reputation with your banker as a good credit risk, so that if a business or money-making opportunity comes your way, you can get the credit necessary to grab it.

About the Author

William Beaver currently lives in Kuwait, where he operates the Black Belt Institute and publishes a Web site/electronic magazine called *Overseas Digest Online* (http://overseasdigest.com) for Americans living abroad. He earned a master of arts degree in philosophy from Miami University and a bachelor of arts degree in philosophy from Ashland University.